W9-CFQ-281

Divine Daisy

a Transpersonal Tale

Written by Bud McClure
Illustrations by Ginny Maki

Divine Daisy A Transpersonal Tale

Photograph of Ginny Maki by Caitlin Longley
Photograph of Bud McClure by Laura Eagin

Published by:
Bumblebee Hollow Press
502 Carlton Avenue
Cloquet, MN 55720
218-879-3243
www.bumblebeehollowpress.com

Library of Congress Control Number: 2009910524

ISBN 978-0-615-32622-1

Printed in Canada by Friesens

10 9 8 7 6 5 4 3 2 1

For Deb and the newest litter of special pups:
Charis, Zoe, Ryder, and Carter.

Every 100 years or so, as legend has it, a very special dog is born into the world. And so it was, one chilly March day in Northern Wisconsin, a Labrador retriever was born into a litter with her four sisters. At first glance there appeared to be nothing uncommon about her. She was neither bigger nor smaller than the rest of the pups and, like her sisters, for the first week after her birth she rooted and nestled close to her mother. But specialness comes in all shapes and sizes and cannot be seen with the naked eye. What makes a dog uniquely special is something inside that shines through in a dog's character. The legend goes on to say that the dog's special gift is awakened only if she is kissed by a rabbit. So you can understand why these dogs are so rare.

Over the weeks, as the pups grew bigger, they ventured around the barn playing on the fresh hay that covered the floor. Sometimes one of the pups would get covered up and hide from the others until her squeal revealed her hiding place. Their mother watched them closely and made sure each night before she went to sleep that they were all accounted for. If you had watched the pups play together you would have noticed that the special one was the shyest. She liked to play with her sisters, but sometimes she seemed overwhelmed by their rough-and-tumble ways. Mostly, she just stayed by her mother's side and napped as her sisters explored the far corners of the barn.

Therefore, it was most surprising that one day, when the dogs were about five weeks old, the special puppy wandered off through the open barn door, into the woods on the other side of the farm. As the pup wandered around the woods exploring all the new sights and barking at all the new sounds, she lost her way back to the barn.

She didn't realize it until very late in the day when the sun began to set in the west. As darkness covered the woods the little pup began to whimper for her mother. She was scared now and realized that she was all alone. She whimpered louder but her mother, who could not hear her, did not come.

What happened next would surprise most people, especially grown-ups, who don't remember the magic of how the universe works. As the puppy whimpered and cried louder and louder, a mother rabbit in her nearby den perked up her big, floppy ears. She heard the pup and knew just what those cries meant. Leaving her own young babies safely tucked in their nest she scurried toward the sound of the pup and found her huddled underneath a large leafy plant. The pup was chilled and shaking. Ever so gently the mother rabbit reached down and picked her up by the nape of her neck.

She carried the pup back to her nest and tenderly placed the puppy in the midst of her own babies. The pup was immediately warmed, tucked in among all that soft rabbit fur. She snuggled deeper among the bunnies and felt safe and secure. The bunnies moved closer to her and, just before they all fell asleep, the mother rabbit leaned down and kissed each one goodnight. Then she kissed the young pup.

Early the next morning, just after the sun popped into the sky, the mother rabbit fed the little ones. Next, she made sure they were sheltered in the nest as she prepared to take the pup back to her own mother in the barn. Picking the pup up she carried her lightly in her mouth and the two of them began the trek through the woods, across the farm, toward the red barn door. As they approached the barn from a distance, there in the doorway sat the pup's worried mother. When the dog saw the rabbit and her puppy she raced toward them leaping high over the wooden fence that stood at the boundary of the farm property. Upon reaching them she stopped and stood wagging her tail. It was a moment of grace as she and the rabbit looked at one another. Then the mother rabbit stood on her hind legs and handed the wayward pup back to her own mother. The dog turned and carried the little one back toward the barn where her four sisters waited.

In a nearby town a little boy was sad. Two weeks ago his last brother had gone back to college and the boy was alone again with just his parents in the big, old house. Three years earlier, his oldest brother had graduated from college and was now working in a far-away city. His brothers had been the center of his life and now they were gone and his heart was aching. His parents worried about him. He mostly stayed in his room and played with his toys. What to do? The boy's parents were not sure. They talked about his loneliness and agreed that sometimes when a heart is hurting it is best to allow it to slowly mend itself. In this way the heart is strengthened and able to tolerate other heartbreaks that would surely follow in life.

But with one so young, the parents thought, perhaps they could find him a companion while letting him grow at the same time. Strangely enough, or maybe not, it was just at that moment in their conversation that the boy's father, who had been holding the newspaper on his lap, looked down to see an ad for the sale of puppies. He read it immediately to the boy's mother and when he had finished, and at exactly the same moment, they both smiled.

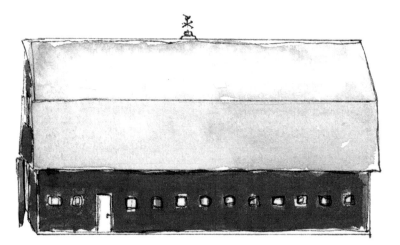

Three weeks later, when the puppies were ready to be weaned from their mother, the boy and his parents drove into the country. The parents told the boy only that they were going on an adventure and along the way there may be a surprise for him. They drove for more than an hour before arriving at the farm. The farmer, who was standing in the driveway, waved to them and pointed toward the barn. The father parked the car near the red barn door. The little boy could immediately hear the commotion inside as the five puppies, who were now eight weeks old, rough-housed with one another.

The farmer slid the big door open and the puppies tumbled out into the yard. At once the boy ran toward the dogs. They yelped and jumped on him, knocking him to the ground. He squealed and laughed as he wrestled with them and became entangled in their twenty legs. Slowly the dogs calmed down and the boy began to look at each one closely. His parents told him that he could take one of the puppies home to live with him. How would he decide? For almost an hour he played with the pups, but each puppy seemed like the right one. Then in a brief moment, that most people would miss, the special pup and the boy looked one another squarely in the eye. And in that briefest of moments, when all sound ceased, both the boy and the dog knew they would be life-long companions. The boy reached out to the pup who ran closer and began licking the boy on his face. The boy's heart was filled with joy and he hugged the puppy and held on for dear life.

Back home that night the father placed the puppy in a cardboard box in the kitchen and the boy's mother arranged a sleeping bag next to it for the little boy. The boy and the puppy fell quickly asleep. The next morning the boy's parents asked him to give the puppy a name, and without a moment's pause the boy said, "Daisy." So began their life together.

Early each morning the mother would let Daisy out into the back yard. Once outside she scampered around to the boy's window, and would paw at the glass until the boy woke up and came outside to play with her.

The boy would take walks with Daisy in the woods near his home. They played fetch, and he took her swimming down in the pond, which was her favorite thing to do. The boy even read his books to Daisy as she sat next to him wagging her tail. Over the days and weeks that followed, as Daisy grew bigger, and learned all about her new home, she began to observe the family of rabbits who lived under the old sauna building in the back yard. With each day that passed Daisy spent more time watching the rabbits come and go. Sometimes she would sit in the yard near the old building and other times she would lie, stretched out, on the back deck keeping an eye on the rabbits at play.

Now, rabbits and dogs have not always been the best
of friends and rabbits are fearful of dogs.
But that specialness of Daisy, that the boy felt
too, made the rabbits trust her and feel safe in her presence.
One day as Daisy sat watching them, one of the younger rabbits
hopped up to her and placed his nose next to hers. For a few
minutes they just lay there, the two of them nose to nose. The boy
watched with fascination, as did the other rabbits who had gathered
in the yard. Suddenly the young rabbit made a sound and the other rabbits
joined in. And then, as if choreographed by some mysterious force, the dog
and the young rabbit rose as one and ran together toward the other rabbits.

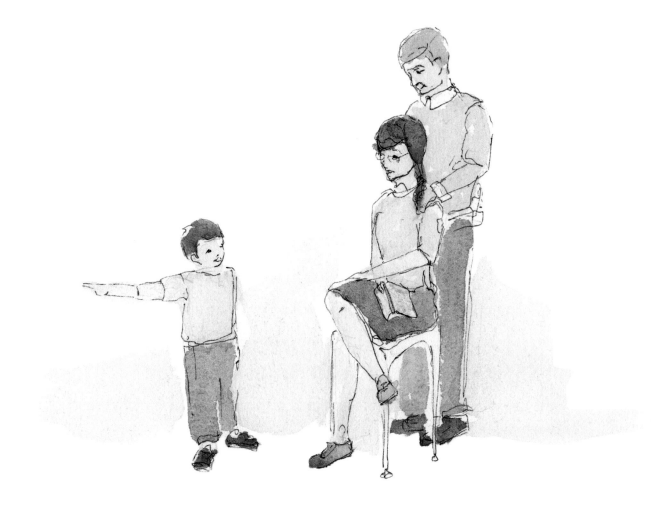

From that moment forward Daisy spent much of her days playing with the rabbits to the delight of the boy who sometimes chased the rabbits around the yard with Daisy. Strangely, or maybe not, the boy was the only one to ever witness this relationship between the dog and her furry friends. When his parents were around, the dog and the rabbits kept a respectful distance. The boy tried to tell his parents about the special relationship, but mostly his parents politely smiled and nodded their heads. They were glad that he was happy again, and that was all that mattered to them. Sometimes grown-ups cannot see what cannot be explained. They have lost their wonder about the vast mysterious world. Instead, they have settled for a reasoned approach to life, satisfied to limit experiences to that which is easily understood.

Over the next three years, Daisy developed a close kinship with the rabbits. She was accepted as one of their family. All of the young rabbits loved Daisy and many a day they could be found sitting on top of her as she lay warming herself in the early afternoon sun. In turn, Daisy looked after them, making sure they didn't wander too far from home or cross the big highway just down the road.

Most days they played their favorite game, tug-of-war, in which the rabbits lined up against Daisy and tried to pull her over to their side of the grass. Once in a while, if Daisy was tired, and there were enough rabbits tugging on the old vine they were able to move her just a little bit. Playing this game always brought the loudest noises from the rabbits and sometimes when the game was over Daisy would bark with them.

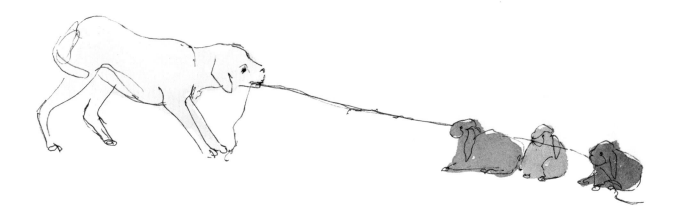

Because she was so trusted, and like them in many ways, the rabbits shared their secrets with her. The first thing they taught Daisy was how to talk with them. Rabbits communicate in a kind of sign language that has developed over many generations. They do this by twitching their noses in different directions. There are actually twenty-six distinct movements that in combination allow rabbits to talk with one another about anything. Because Daisy had a nose similar to the rabbits, it was fairly easy for her to learn how to talk with them. The second thing that Daisy learned was the reason that rabbits have big floppy ears. Their ears have grown big because rabbits have learned to hear and understand all other animal languages.

They have become skilled at comprehending what other animals are talking about. Rabbits are mostly quiet, because they are listening to everything that is going on around them. Daisy's ears were similar to the rabbits, but it was difficult for her to learn how to hear other languages. Daisy also learned that rabbits' ears are floppy because it helps them land softly after they have taken a big hop. When the rabbits hop their ears float up like little parachutes and insure them of a gentle landing. Now Daisy had fairly big ears but when she tried jumping off the deck her ears didn't help soften her landing one bit. The rabbits made lots of noise as they watched Daisy jump off the deck with her ears outstretched.

The last thing Daisy learned was the best of all. Everyone will be surprised to know this secret. The only noise or sound that rabbits make is one of laughter. Everything else they communicate with their noses, but for some strange reason, or maybe not, laughter is never silent. In return for sharing their secrets with her, Daisy taught the rabbits to swim. Late in the afternoon, when the summer sun was hottest, Daisy would lead the rabbits down the wooded path to the local pond. There, she and the rabbits would run as fast as they could and, together, leap into the water creating a giant splash.

Sometimes in life everything is just the way we want it to be. Sometimes life seems so perfect that we want those times to last forever. Life was that way for the boy now and his parents, and it was that way for Daisy and the rabbits. But life is full of surprises and when we least expect it, things change.

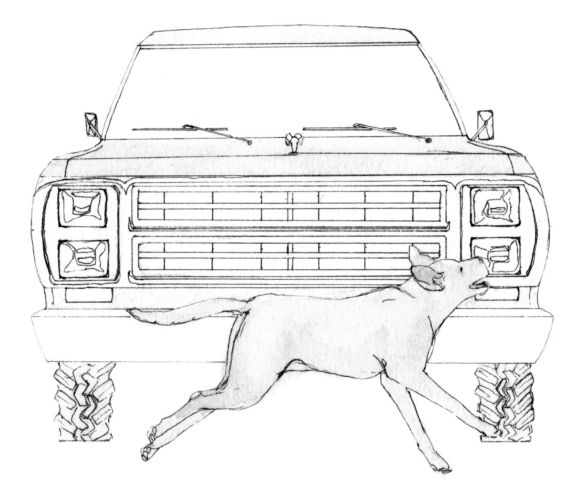

One day as Daisy lay on the deck watching the young rabbits play she noticed that one of the youngest was missing. She sat up and scanned the yard but she couldn't see the little rabbit. Worried, she climbed down and began searching the nearby woods. The rabbit seemed to be nowhere around. Daisy's instinct told her that something was wrong and she widened her search by heading down the road to look for the rabbit. As she approached the big highway, she was alarmed when she saw the little rabbit in the middle of the road. To his left, unseen by the young rabbit, was a large truck speeding toward him. Daisy raced toward the highway. Running faster than she ever had before, she reached the road, dashed across it and in one moment, that seemed to last a long time, two things happened. With one long stride Daisy snatched the rabbit by the nape of his neck and with all her strength tossed him safely to the other side. And in that same moment the truck struck Daisy with such a force that she too was tossed up into the air landing in the grass by the side of the road.

What followed cannot be adequately described with words, because there are no words, in any language, that can convey the depth of sorrow and grief that the boy and his parents and the rabbits were about to experience. Nor are there any words that can soften or make acceptable the harsh reality that Daisy was dead. In the moments that followed there was such silence that one could easily imagine the world standing still. And in that moment all of the rabbits in the warren sensed that something terrible had happened. From under the old sauna building, from the yard, and from the woods they all raced toward the highway where they found Daisy lying. They gathered closely around her touching her body as if to protect her. Some laid flowers around her and they waited there alongside the highway with her.

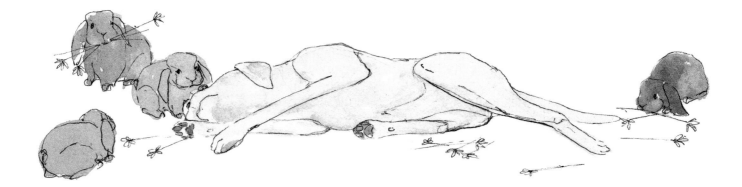

A bit later the boy began calling Daisy to come into the house. She had

been outside most of the day and it was nearing suppertime. However, she

did not come. He called her name again and again but she did not appear.

The boy told his mother and the two of them went out into the yard looking for Daisy.

The boy searched the woods and the mother walked down the road looking for her.

As she approached the highway she saw the group of rabbits standing and sitting on the

far side of the road. She hadn't seen any thing like that before. It was then she caught

a glimpse of the golden form lying silently in their midst. Without taking one more step

her heart sank so fast that she gasped for breath. The rush of tears came so suddenly

that she could barely make her way to the dog. Upon reaching Daisy's side she fell to

her knees and held the dog. The rabbits silently retreated and watched as the boy's

mother wept.

When the boy learned of Daisy's death, and later saw the limp body of his dog he was grief stricken. His parents held him as he cried. The next day the family buried Daisy near the old sauna, under the shade of a giant maple tree. They placed a small stone marker on her grave. The shadow cast by the tree comforted the three of them as they sat by the grave holding onto one another. An hour passed before the parents stood up and walked slowly back to the house. The boy stayed at Daisy's graveside and one by one the rabbits began to gather around him. Together they sat and each in their own way remembered Daisy. When such a tragedy occurs in our life we look for a reason as to why it has happened. We are left numb and sometimes angry when we realize that there are never any satisfactory explanations that could lessen our heartache. And we wonder how we can survive. But survive we do and as we grieve and slowly recover, we learn that life goes on.

Now this is not quite the end of this tale, because life did go on. Six months later something so out of the ordinary happened that only the rabbits and the boy had the ability to recognize the truth of what they were to witness. Early one morning as the boy lay sleeping he heard a noise outside that woke him up. Still a bit sleepy he opened his eyes and saw a large rabbit pawing at his window. He thought he was dreaming because when he looked closer he thought he recognized the rabbit. Its fur had a golden hue. But when the boy looked into the rabbit eyes he knew who she was. He jumped out of bed and raced upstairs, out the back door and into the yard.

He fell to his knees. The rabbit leaped into his arms
and licked his face, and the boy held on for dear life.

Creating Divine Daisy

We owned a magical dog once and she was the inspiration for this book. The story itself came to me in a series of early morning images that appeared over a period of months. No matter how hard I tried to ignore them they continued to re-appear with a vividness that compelled me to act. I outlined the story and then began looking for an illustrator who could bring the story to life.

After a futile two-month search I wandered into a student exhibit at the Tweed Museum in Duluth and was immediately captivated by the artwork of Ginny Maki. I contacted her and briefly described the story to her and without a moment's hesitation she joined the project. Her initial drawings had an uncanny, even eerie resemblance to those first images that had haunted me months earlier. The writing process that followed was joyful as the story flowed through me almost verbatim as it appears in the book today.

Acknowledgements

Thanks to everyone who participated in the process of creating this book: Molly McClure, Kim Robinson, and Nicole Schmidt who offered valuable feedback on the manuscript. Beth Bartlett whose careful editing and insight into the spiritual nature of this book made it better. Sandy Woolum who always finds a creative way to resolve the unresolvable. Jennifer Gordon who worked with me on the original design of the book. Laura Eagin, from the Savanna College of Art and Design, who made it all fit together so that the finished product was much greater than the sum of its parts. Finally, thanks to Lisa Fitzpatrick and the staff at the Visualization and Digital Imaging Lab where the design of this book took place.

A very special thank you to Ginny Maki who brought Divine Daisy to life with her illustrations. She was the perfect partner in this project and her beautiful artwork speaks for itself.